EXCITING STORIES
FOR BRAVE BOYS

Exciting Stories for Brave Boys

An Inspiring Book About Courage, Friendship and Helping Others

Mia Anderson

Liberstax Publishing, London, United Kingdom.

© Copyright 2022 - All rights reserved.

by Mia Anderson

Cover design by Sam Art Studio

The content contained within this book may not be reproduced, duplicated or transmitted without direct written permission from the author or the publisher.

Under no circumstances will any blame or legal responsibility be held against the publisher, or author, for any damages, reparation, or monetary loss due to the information contained within this book, either directly or indirectly.

Legal Notice:

This book is copyright protected. It is only for personal use. You cannot amend, distribute, sell, use, quote or paraphrase any part, or the content within this book, without the consent of the author or publisher.

Disclaimer Notice:

Please note the information contained within this document is for educational and entertainment purposes only. All effort has been executed to present accurate, up to date, reliable, complete information. No warranties of any kind are declared or implied. Readers acknowledge that the author is not engaged in the rendering of legal, financial, medical or professional advice. The content within this book has been derived from various sources. Please consult a licensed professional before attempting any techniques outlined in this book.

By reading this document, the reader agrees that under no circumstances is the author responsible for any losses, direct or indirect, that are incurred as a result of the use of the information contained within this document, including, but not limited to, errors, omissions, or inaccuracies.

CONTENTS

Introduction 8

The First Day of School 10

Aiming for A's 23

Icky Lizzy 37

For the Win 55

The Greatest Diwali Dinner 69

Down the Hill 89

The Dental Treatment Delay 101

The Feather of Truth 117

Introduction

When times are tough and the stakes are high, we can all be

Bold

Remarkable

Authentic

Virtuous

Electric

in our own special ways.

Facing fears and learning new things is part of life's journey.

We can close our eyes and take ten deep breaths to discover our strengths from within.

Let's hone our talents little by little to become better people each day.

The First Day of School

The sun shone brightly on a glorious September morning in New Jersey. The air was clean and crisp, while the birds fluttered overhead, chirping merry tunes. The American suburb was a picture-perfect sight for anybody who came out for a stroll—all except for Jack Campbell.

The young boy sulked as he waited by the bus stop, dreading the big, yellow school bus heading his way. It was his first day as a third grader, and he was far from excited. In fact, he would have stayed in bed and played with his action figures if his mother allowed it. Jack was bright, kind, and playful. But above all things, he was extremely timid and shy. He detested facing new people more than anything in the world. First days of school always meant being in a new class and having to make new friends.

To that, he grumbled, "Where's a big brother when you need him the most? Why did Jeff have to leave for middle school?"

Jack kept his head down, hoping the bus would head past the stop sign. Instead, it came to a safe halt before him.

"Come aboard, boy," the driver hollered as the doors swung open.

Jack took a deep breath, pulled his hat down, and climbed up. To his dismay, everyone turned silent the moment he walked on. Jack tried his best to hide the shiver in his knees as he strode past a bunch of fresh faces watching his every move. After what seemed like an eternity, the shy boy eventually made his way to the end.

Jack ducked behind the backseat, hiding himself from everybody's gaze.

"This is the worst day ever," he mumbled under his breath, slumping his bag beside him.

As he looked out the window, he couldn't help but envy a lone racoon scampering down the sidewalk.

"Lucky thing. I bet they don't have problems making new friends."

The children's chattering was drowned by the engine's humming as the bus took off again. Jack chose to sit quietly in his corner. With no one to talk to, he amused himself by counting every tree and bush that passed by. Soon, he started to grow bored.

Six more blocks until we arrive at school. That's going to be a while, he thought. *It's a good thing I came prepared.*

He looked around to check if anyone was watching him. When the coast was clear, he slowly reached into his bag and smiled as he pulled out an action figure.

"Hello, Galaxyman," Jack whispered, admiring his favorite superhero toy.

The figurine donned a silver suit and had a bright red cape clipped to its shoulders. Jack swooshed it around. For the first time that morning, he felt happy.

Suddenly, the bus jolted, and everyone jerked forward. The children held their breath as they clung to their seats. Murmurs filled the air when the vehicle halted. The driver hurried down the aisle with worry written all over his face.

"I'm sorry, kids. Darn raccoon ran across the street! I had to stop the bus because I didn't want to squish the poor fella," he said. "Is everyone alright?"

Fortunately, no one was hurt. But Jack had other problems.

He'd lost his grip on the action figure. His eyes widened when he saw his toy sitting at the foot of a seat three rows forward. He had to get it before the bus took off again. However, that meant talking to the other kids. Jack closed his eyes and took a deep breath. But before he could get up, he found a boy his age standing before him.

"Is this yours?" The stranger asked, holding out Jack's Galaxyman action figure.

Jack nodded.

"Thanks," he mumbled, taking it back.

"No problem," the boy answered.

There was an awkward moment of silence before the stranger spoke again.

"I'm Mike, by the way. I think we're in the same grade, but we've never been in the same class. What's your name?"

"I'm Jack," he muttered, fumbling the toy in his hands.

Mike nodded and smiled as he said, "I think it's cool that you like Galaxyman. I'm a big fan too. My favorite's Starboy, the sidekick."

Jack instantly felt excitement stirring inside of him. Despite his fear of making new friends, he imagined how fun it would be to have someone to talk to on the ride to school. Mike seemed like a nice guy. Plus, he enjoyed playing with action figures too!

With all his might, Jack summoned the courage to ask, "Do you want to sit with me and play?"

It didn't take a second for Mike to answer, "Sounds great! I've got my Starboy action figure in my bag."

Mike hurried to fetch his things and made it back just in time for the bus to take off again. Then they started to play.

"Emergency! There's a planet being attacked by evil aliens! What should we do, Galaxyman?" Mike warned, trying to hide the excitement in his voice.

"Save the galaxy, of course!" Jack replied in a deep tone.

For some reason, the boys felt like they had known each other their whole lives. They were so caught up in the game that they didn't realize the bus already arrived at school. They couldn't care less about being the last to get off the bus, nor did they mind if they looked quite quirky swinging their toys around in the air.

As soon as they entered the front doors, they rushed toward the bulletin board and cheered when they found out they were in the same class.

Maybe today won't be so bad after all, Jack thought, feeling more than content to walk side by side with his new friend.

Jack learned that talking to others wasn't such a terrible feat. In fact, sharing ideas with someone else made school more enjoyable. From that moment on, Jack promised to be more open to meeting new people and making new friends.

Aiming for A's

Minho Park was an extremely diligent fifth grader. He strove for perfection and left no room for excuses. His friends and teachers always gushed about how responsible and mature he was for such a young boy. But deep down, he was trying his best to prove himself to his family.

Minho's older brother, Suho, was a marvelous achiever. His parents were so pleased that they built a glass case in the living room to display his medals, trophies, and diplomas. Minho looked up to Suho—his beloved *hyung*—and couldn't imagine a world without him. However, there were times when he couldn't help but feel his achievements were worth less compared to his.

To make up for it, Minho studied day and night—even on the weekends—just so he could get straight A's.

He even plotted his calendars just so he could keep track of his progress. With all his hard work, he easily made it to the top of every class, except for one subject he struggled to pass with flying colors: Foreign language.

Being born and raised in Seoul meant that he spoke and wrote flawless Korean. However, English came as a challenge.

Being the hardworking boy that he was, Minho put in extra hours to sharpen his skills. But every time he opened the book, he found himself struggling harder than before. His tongue coiled, twisted, and stiffened as he uttered every word. On top of all that, his grammar was completely off point.

There are no excuses, Minho thought, gripping his hair as he stared at his notes. *I must ace that exam tomorrow. I must make my family proud.*

***

To his dismay, the poor boy nearly cried when he received his grade during class.

"I got a D?" He gasped wildly, gripping the test paper.

It was absolutely dreadful!

Not only did he earn strange stares from everyone in the room, but now all his classmates knew that he was close to failing English. Minho didn't feel any better when the teacher announced a makeup exam for those who didn't do well enough. Instead, he shrank in his seat until the period ended.

When the school bell rang, Minho grabbed his things and rushed out the door. He ran as fast as his legs could take him into the hall, down the stairs, and across the school grounds. Tears blurred his sight as he raced down the sidewalk. He couldn't care less about where he was going. Soon, he found himself alone in a dark, dank alley a few blocks away from school.

Consumed by rage, Minho took the English book out of his bag and threw it at a nearby garbage bin. Then he slumped to the ground, defeated.

"Why am I not good enough?" He sobbed.

The more he tried to calm himself, the more his chest tightened with worry. Tears streamed endlessly from his small eyes. Before he knew it, they grew sore and began to droop. Then sleep took over his weary mind.

Minho tossed and turned on the cold ground, haunted by the horrors of his low mark. He mumbled, "Why? Why?" while pulling his schoolbag close to his chest. As he was lost in his dreams, night came swiftly over the city.

The grief-stricken child woke to rattling, rumbling, and screeching in an alley that was now darker than ever. He sat up in panic as his thoughts raced with scary fantasies of what lurked in the corners of the street. He closed his eyes and held his breath.

Just when he felt like crumbling in fear, a blinding light swept through the alleyway.

"Minho? Are you here?" Called a familiar voice.

"Yes! It's me!" He yelled, scrambling to his feet.

Minho beamed at the sight of Suho—his beloved *hyung*.

"What are you doing here?" Suho asked. "I was supposed to pick you up from school. I've been looking all over for you! Mom and Dad are worried sick!"

Minho bowed his head and sniffled. "I'm sorry. I got a D in English even though I studied really hard. I felt so upset, so I ran away."

"You don't have to beat yourself up for that," his *hyung* assured. "It's not the end of the world, Minho."

"You're wrong, *hyung*. I have to get straight A's," Minho grumbled. "You're so smart and talented. I want to be awesome like you. I have to be."

There was a moment of silence before Minho felt his brother's arms around him.

"Minho, you're the most amazing little brother anyone could ask for. You're smart, funny, and super talented in your own special way. I'm not going to love you less if you don't get straight A's. But if you really want to ace English, I'd be more than happy to help."

Minho smiled gratefully while his *hyung* gathered all of his things—even the cast-off English book. Then they headed home.

***

Minho's parents fussed over him the moment he arrived. He was rushed into a warm bath and was dried and dressed in comfy clothes after. His mother prepared a delicious meal of steamed rice, fried dumplings, and bean sprouts—his favorite. Then the Park family gathered around the table for dinner.

After helping their mother wash the dishes, Minho and his *hyung* headed into the bedroom for a quick round of studying.

It was nothing like Minho expected.

His *hyung* was cheerful, witty, and joked around at every chance he got. He turned the study session into a gameshow, which Minho played as the prime contestant. Minho was having so much fun that he forgot how much he dreaded English. Instead, he found himself giggling out the right answers to every question.

Minho and his *hyung* did this every night for a week until the day of the makeup exam. After all his hard work, Minho felt more than ready to take the test.

***

Once he received his grade, Minho took the first bus home and dashed into the living room, proudly waving a test paper in the air.

"I got an A!" He exclaimed.

Everyone was delighted to hear the news. His *hyung* cheered, hoisting Minho on his shoulders. His parents quickly searched for a spare frame to put the test paper in. They displayed Minho's achievement above the glass case for everyone to see.

Minho learned that getting good grades didn't have to be a struggle. Rather, learning was supposed to be an enjoyable and nourishing experience. Tackling lessons bit by bit every day was a sure way to let the knowledge sink in.

Acing that English test was the most victorious Minho had ever felt—and he owed it all to his amazing *hyung* who was with him till the end.

I WILL GROW HAPPILY

Icky Lizzy

Tom Robinson was a kind and thoughtful boy. He lived with his mother and grandmother in a small apartment just outside the city of London in England. He always looked forward to spending time with his family, especially on the weekends. However, all that changed when he began his seventh year.

Since he was growing up, his mother and grandmother thought it would be great for him to spend more time with boys his age. So, they sent him to an all-boys boarding school in the country. By stroke of fate, Tom met Hugh and Daniel, who quickly became his closest friends. In their funny little ways, they convinced him that girls were a whole different species.

"Girls are icky," Hugh whispered, scrunching his nose. "All they do is braid their hair and talk about shoes."

"Be careful when you're around them," Daniel added. "Because they'll drag you into playing their boring games. Then when you least expect it, they'll turn you into one of them!"

This shocked Tom at first. But the more he thought about it, the more he realized that girls and guys dressed, talked, and moved differently. As Tom grew wary, he felt that boarding school—apart from his home—was the safest place to be.

Little did he know he was in for a big surprise.

***

"How was school, love?" His mother asked, picking him up on the weekend.

"It was great, Mum. I made lots of new friends," he answered. "I'm also doing pretty well in Math and History."

"Wow, you've been busy!" she said, passing him a box of his grandmother's Danish butter cookies. "I think you deserve a break. I've got the perfect thing planned tonight to start it off."

"Tell me, Mum!" He exclaimed, munching on the sweets.

"Do you remember Lizzy from kindergarten?" She asked, starting the car. "She's turning 11 today, and her mother invited all of us to come over for dinner. Isn't that exciting?"

"Can you say that again, Mum?" He asked, hoping he misheard her over the engine.

"A birthday party, dear." She repeated. "You were such great friends! I remember how much you loved playing on the swings together after school."

Suddenly, Tom felt his stomach squirming. Lizzy was a girl! She was the kind of person his friends warned him to stay away from. Apart from his mother and grandmother, Tom had no experience talking to girls. To his dismay, he couldn't come up with an excuse good enough to get him out of this sticky situation.

Poor Tom sunk in his seat, panicking in silence.

His mother drove by their apartment to pick up his grandmother and the present. Then they headed to the party.

***

Lizzy's birthday was held at the local park. The venue was decorated with bright balloons, checkered picnic blankets, and a huge banner that said, "Lizzy's Spectacular 11th." String lights hung from tree to tree, while lively music filled the air. Apart from a long table lined with chicken sandwiches, potato salad, and meat pies, Lizzy's father stood by the grill, whipping up a delicious barbecue.

Tom gripped the gift tightly and hid behind his family as they approached the birthday girl.

"Happy birthday, Lizzy!" Tom's mother and grandmother said.

"Happy birthday," Tom mumbled, handing her the present.

"Thank you," Lizzy chirped.

She wore a pretty blue dress and a bright purple headband. She had the same pale, green eyes and dimpled cheeks. However, she turned out to be much taller than Tom expected.

As Tom and Lizzy's families chatted away, he caught her staring at him. He tried his best to hold her gaze. Their eyes locked for a good ten seconds. Then she gave him a funny smile.

Tom looked away before she could speak.

Hugh and Daniel were right. I should be careful around girls. Lizzy's making fun of me, he thought.

His fear grew when he spotted dozens of little girls running around the playground. His mind raced as he imagined each young lady as a cruel, boy-eating monster. Tom longed to be back in the dorms, surrounded by all his guy friends. He was lost in a trance until a tap on his shoulder snapped him back to reality.

Tom noticed his mother and grandmother walking away with Lizzy's parents. And to his horror, five of Lizzy's friends came and stood behind her.

They were all girls! Plus, they smiled funnily at him just like Lizzy did earlier.

Sweat trickled down his forehead as they stared at him. Tom's thoughts froze. He felt like fainting. He wished they would all disappear.

To make things worse, Lizzy stepped closer to ask, "Would you like to play with us?"

Tom opened his mouth to speak. But he only managed a squeal.

I can't take this. There's too many of them, he panicked.

Soon, he found himself running away.

"Get him!" The girls screamed in chorus, racing after him.

The chase was intense!

Tom's heart raced when he heard giggling and footsteps closely behind. He sprinted across the swings and leaped over the sandbox as fast as he could. Then he escaped into a nearby thicket. When he thought he was far enough from Lizzy and her friends, he huddled behind a bush, held his knees close, and gasped for air.

Tom crossed his fingers, hoping he was finally alone. But the strange silence was far from comforting. Before he knew it, he found himself falling to the ground when Lizzy appeared behind him, gripping his shoulders.

"Boo!" She screamed.

"Great," Tom yelped.

"Hey, are you alright?" she asked, holding her hand out to help him. "You look pale."

"Just stay away from me!" he answered.

He spoke too soon to realize the harshness in his voice. But Lizzy noticed it right away.

"What's gotten into you? You're not the nice boy I played with in kindergarten," she sighed.

Without thinking twice, Tom snapped, "I've changed."

To that, Lizzie answered, "I preferred the old you."

For the first time in a long while, he looked Lizzy straight in the eyes. Only then did he realize they were swelling with tears. As he watched her walk away, Tom felt his heart clench. He knew he did something wrong.

It didn't help when Lizzy turned around to shout, "Oh yeah, I was only giggling at you because you had cookie crumbs on your chin! I wanted to tell you, but you never listened!"

Tom felt guilty and incredibly mean. He knew he had to make amends right away.

"Wait, Lizzy! I'm sorry," he sighed, grabbing her by the elbow. "I didn' mean to be rude. The truth is, I was really afraid of talking to you."

"I'm not a bad person, you know," Lizzy whispered.

"I know," Tom answered. "I'm really sorry."

There was a moment of silence before he summoned the courage to ask, "I'd really like to play with you and your friends."

Tom was relieved to see Lizzy's frown turn into a pretty smile. In an instant, he found himself being dragged by the hand into the playground.

Tom never expected to enjoy the birthday party. He joined in all the games, filled his belly with delicious food, and made a whole bunch of new friends. He didn't mind that they were girls. In fact, he found each of them to be funny, witty, and exciting in their own special ways. After dinner, he found himself begging his mother to stay a little longer, just so he could play with Lizzy on the swings. The two friends laughed and chatted while they watched the guests leave.

As the night breeze blew through his sweater, Tom realized that he learned a very important life lesson. Although guys and girls had their own unique traits, there was no reason to treat people differently. In the end, Tom realized that it was perfectly alright to befriend girls. Getting to know people was an adventure—and the best part was that each person was unique!

Lizzy was a special childhood friend whom he vowed to treasure for as long as he could. And boy, he couldn't wait to see the shocked look on Hugh and Daniel's faces when they learned how much fun they had at her spectacular birthday party!

For the Win

Brazilians love football. In fact, it's their national sport. It's a wonderful game that brings people of all ages together. It's also a fun way to get some exercise. Football can be played as a hobby. But it could also turn into a thrilling and fulfilling job for very committed players.

It was almost every boy's dream to play professional football when they got older—and Alejandro wasn't an exemption.

He was small and skinny compared to other twelve-year-olds. But he had a lot of heart. He lived, breathed, and played football like his life depended on it.

He thought of football as a dance. He practiced his footwork during his spare time to get his moves perfect. Because of his hard work, he turned out to be one of the best dribblers on his middle school's football team—*Os Defensores*. Although they were never in the lead, they did fairly well during most interschool competitions.

All until this year.

Apart from Alejandro, who played as the attacking midfielder, and Sebastian, the goalkeeper, the team had a new lineup. This meant everyone still had to train hard to reach the top of their game. Above everything, some members didn't know how to play to each other's strengths. They spent months running through drills and coming up with winning strategies. Unfortunately, their best wasn't good enough to snag any victory cup.

Alejandro loved a challenge. But he never expected his team to lose 3 matches in a row. Today, they played against the *Piratas*, who led the game 1-0.

Alejandro stood at centerfield with a freshly scraped knee. He felt sick seeing ten more seconds on the clock till halftime. It didn't help that their opponents were bigger and faster. He detested how slim their chances were of winning. His teammates on the field were equally pale with worry. But Alejandro knew they couldn't give up.

He waited until the other team's midfielder came close enough. Then he dropped his shoulders, swooped down, and circled his foot around the ball. Once he stole it, he ran across the field on his toes, dodging past the other team's defenses. He kicked the ball with all his might. To his relief, he scored a goal.

At that moment, the clock stopped for halftime. Now, the score was even.

As soon as the referee blew the whistle, Os Defensores regrouped by the benches.

"Good shot, Alejandro," their coach, *Treinador* Tomas, applauded.

"Thanks," Alejandro muttered, breathless.

Alejandro felt a mixture of excitement and dread as his team huddled up. He knew winning would be even more challenging now that *Piratas* would be raising their game.

"Guys, we need a better plan," Sebastian said. "We're barely making it out of this game alive."

"He's right. We need to work together on this," Alejandro seconded.

Everyone nodded. But when the coach asked, "How would you like to play this out?"

Nobody said a word.

"Come on, guys. You must have an idea," Alejandro encouraged.

It took a while for anybody to speak up until Julio, a wingback, answered meekly, "You're the best amongst us. We'll do anything you ask."

"Yeah, anything," the team chorused.

Alejandro and Sebastian looked at each other, puzzled. This wasn't what teamwork was about—it was no wonder they weren't playing like a well-oiled machine. Alejandro felt sorry for the newer members who felt quite unsure of themselves on the field.

Alejandro knew that he and Sebastian needed to make them believe in themselves and each other in order to win this game.

"It's not about who's the best. It's about being the best together," Alejandro said, breaking the silence.

He nudged Sebastian, who quickly added, "He's right. We've got to be more comfortable around each other to stand a chance against *Piratas*. So, don't be shy."

"Boys, you're doing great. But I know you can achieve greater things if you trust each other," *Treinador* Tomas said.

After a minute of thinking, Umberto, the team's right wingback, offered a suggestion.

"Can I switch to striker? I've been practicing with my brother all summer. I'd really like to give it a shot."

"That's great!" Sebastian cheered. "Does anybody have any hidden talents they'd like to share?"

"I was a pretty good defending midfielder in my previous school," said Dante, a center back.

"I'll switch with you," offered Chris.

Treinador Tomas smiled proudly, saying, "Look at you, boys! Planning like professionals."

"We'll do more than that, *Treinador* Tomas. We're going to play like them!" said Alejandro.

The team chanted as they made their way back to the field. Soon, the game resumed.

As expected, the *Piratas* played like champions. Alejandro and his team found themselves chasing their opponents around for the beginning of the second half. It took a while for them to put their plan into action—let alone steal the ball. But Alejandro was persistent. He went after the *Piratas*, looking to his team for support. Luckily, two of his teammates understood the signal and followed closely behind him. To his delight, Alejandro finally saw an opening. He wasted no time snatching the ball and passing it to Dante.

Dante dribbled it across the field before passing it to Ricky, a center forward. Ricky wasted no time passing it to Alejandro who gave it to Umberto as soon as he saw an opening. Umberto swiftly kicked the ball past the opponent's goalkeeper and scored.

The timer ended. The match was finished. The crowd cheered for the winning team.

Os Defensores shook hands with the *Piratas* and claimed their victory.

Alejandro and his team learned that it was normal to feel nervous during a game. But as long as they had each other's backs, they could achieve great things together. This game taught them the values of trust and perseverance. From that day, *Os Defensores* moved onward with newfound courage and everlasting friendship.

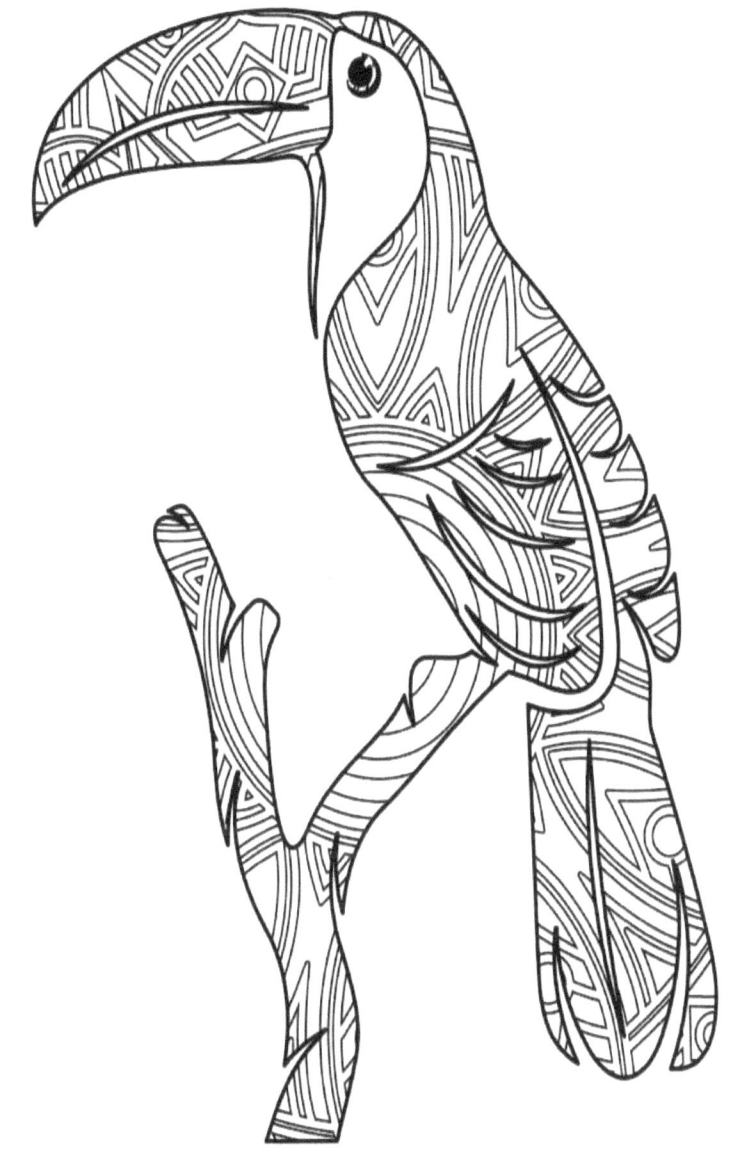

The Greatest Diwali Dinner

Kiaan jumped out of bed on one sunny morning. He wore the biggest smile on his face. He tossed his sheets aside, slipped on his slippers, and ran downstairs. He didn't even bother to comb his hair or to change out of his pajamas. He just wanted the day to begin.

After months of waiting, the first day of *Diwali* finally arrived. It was also known as the Festival of Lights. This was one of the biggest and most important Hindi celebrations—and was certainly Kiaan's favorite.

Diwali is celebrated yearly. However, there is no fixed date for it. The festivities last for five days between mid-October to mid-November, depending on the Hindu calendar. Kiaan loved seeing the village adorned with decorations. He also looked forward to dancing, feasting, and exchanging gifts with his family. But most of all, he longed to see the world sparkle in a beautiful, dreamy glow.

Kiaan couldn't wait to light up the house with candles and lanterns—an ancient tradition that symbolized the victory of goodness over wickedness. He bolted down the stairs, thinking, *this is going to be the best Diwali yet!*

From the landing, he saw his parents, grandparents, and younger sisters gathered around the table for breakfast. He jumped down the last step, yelling, "Happy Diwali, everyone!"

His family turned to him and smiled.

"Good morning, Kiaan," his grandmother greeted. "Happy *Diwali* to you too."

"Come join us for breakfast, dear. You'll need a lot of energy today," his mother called.

Kiaan couldn't hide the skip in his step as he approached the table.

"I know," he gushed. "We're all going to have so much fun!"

He was lost in his thoughts to notice his parents eyeing each other knowingly. He sat beside his father, who handed him a *moong dal ladoo*. The boy happily received the round, sweet treat and scarfed it down.

"So, what should we do first, Baba?" He asked. "Are you taking us to the lake? Are we watching the fireworks tonight? I think we should!"

There was a moment of silence before his father answered, "Actually, your mother and I had something else in mind for you."

Kiaan's eyes brightened as he turned to his mother. He leaned in, eager to hear her speak. Instead, she handed him a piece of paper folded in half. Kiaan opened it and read it right away.

"Black lentils, heavy cream, butter, garam masala, onions, fresh ginger," his voice trailed. He turned to his mother and asked, "What's this?"

"A grocery list, dear," she replied. "Those are things we'll need to make *dal makhani* for tonight."

It was a creamy and flavorful stew that paired perfectly with *naan*—delicious oven-baked flatbread and a family favorite.

"But why are you giving this to me?" he asked, staring at the list.

"Kiaan, dear," his mother answered. "Since you're a big boy now, your father and I believe it might be time for you to learn some responsibility. We're sending you to the supermarket to buy some ingredients for tonight's dinner."

Kiaan's eyes widened.

"Mama! Baba! Are you serious? I can't do that. I've never shopped for food on my own," he gulped.

"There's always a first time for everything, Kiaan," his father said. "Don't be afraid. It's quite simple, actually."

But that didn't calm Kiaan.

"What if I forget something? Or worse—what if I pick up the wrong things?" He said, breathless.

"We trust you, my boy. You'll do perfectly fine," his father assured.

Poor Kiaan sighed, "What if I don't trust myself?"

The room fell silent until his grandmother cleared her throat.

"My dear child," Kiaan's grandmother chuckled. "It's perfectly normal to feel scared before trying something new. What's remarkable is having the courage to put your fears aside and take on the challenge with a clear mind."

"How do I do that?" Kiaan asked.

The old lady smiled as she answered.

"I'll tell you a secret to stay calm in times of trouble. First, close your eyes. Then take five slow breaths. Get in touch with yourself and clear your thoughts. When you open your eyes, you'll find that all your problems can be conquered by your strong will. You can do anything you set your mind to!"

His grandmother's words were quite inspiring. Kiaan was curious to know how he would manage a new challenge. He looked around to see his family eager for his answer.

"I might be able to handle a little grocery shopping," he whispered.

"That's our boy," his father cheered, ruffling his hair.

After breakfast, Kiaan headed upstairs to clean himself up and get dressed. Then he approached his mother who handed him a grocery list and a pouch of money. Kiaan kissed his parents and grandparents goodbye. Soon, he was out the front door.

Kiaan strided down the busy sidewalks, wiggling his way through villagers in a rush. He took a shortcut down a twisted alley and emerged on the other side of the block. To his delight, he finally arrived at the nearest supermarket.

He quickly dusted his shoes and took a basket from the pile. He puffed his chest out and breathed deeply.

"Alright, let's do this," he said, reading the list.

- Black lentils
- Heavy Cream
- Butter
- Garam masala
- Onions
- Fresh ginger

That's six things. This shouldn't be too hard, he thought.

Kiaan headed into the grains section and found packs of black lentils neatly stacked on the rack. He fetched one and stuffed it into his basket.

"Item number one—check!" He said, proudly. "Next stop—the dairy section."

Kiaan strolled to an area lined with massive refrigerators and chillers. His eyes scanned the vast selection of chilled cheese, bottled juices, and boxed milk. Eventually, he found heavy cream displayed beside the whole milk. He put a carton of heavy cream into his basket and checked the list for the next item. To his delight, he spotted some butter displayed on a higher shelf.

"Wow, two things in one go. This is turning out to be a great trip!" he said, putting his shopping list inside the basket next to the heavy cream.

He set the basket on the floor. With full focus, he mounted on a ledge and stretched out as far as he could for a bar of butter.

"Success!" He said, grabbing a gold packet.

Kiaan hopped down, excited to fetch the next item on the list. To his dismay, the paper was soaked and his mother's neat handwriting was completely smudged.

"No! I ruined *Diwali*!" He gasped, trying to read it.

But it was ruined.

"I shouldn't have put the list beside the heavy cream. Now it's all wet! I can't read what's on the paper anymore! Goodness! How I'll never get the shopping done?"

His breath quickened as he imagined his family's disappointment. Just when he felt like giving up, he remembered the advice his grandmother gave him during breakfast. He immediately decided to give it a shot.

"I really hope this works," he mumbled, sinking to the ground and slumping his back on a refrigerator.

Kiaan sat with his legs crossed. He closed his eyes, and took five long breaths. He tried his best to ignore the chatter of other customers. He emptied his mind of bad thoughts and focused on what he could do at the moment.

He chanted, "Black lentils, heavy cream, butter," and repeated it over and over again.

Soon, he remembered the other half of the ingredients on the list.

"Garam masala, onions, and fresh ginger!" He exclaimed, rushing to his feet.

With heightened spirits, he grabbed the basket and hurried around the supermarket to finish the task. After gathering all the items, and checking them twice, he went straight to the cashier to pay. Kiaan arrived home 30 minutes later, smiling from ear to ear as he carried full bags of groceries in each hand. He handed them to his parents, who looked at him with amazement.

"That was quick," his mother said, peeping into the bags.

"You got everything on your first try. You did perfectly, son," his father cheered.

Although part of it was true, Kiaan felt that he didn't deserve that kind of praise.

He bowed his head and said, "Mama, Baba, I have something to confess. Things didn't go so smoothly. The shopping list got wet when I put it beside the carton of heavy cream. Mama's handwriting got smudged, which made it difficult to read. I used grandma's breathing advice to calm myself down and remember what was on the rest of the list. I'm not perfect. I just got lucky."

Kiaan expected his parents to take back their word. But they gave him a big, warm hug instead.

"That's nothing to be sorry for. You were able to clear your mind during a sticky situation. We're very proud of you," his mother said, kissing him on the cheek.

"Your mother's right, son. It really shows that you pay attention and that you care," his father added. "In fact, I think you deserve a reward for showing such strength. Why don't you call your sisters down and bring your kites? I think we've got time before lunch for a few rounds of flying."

Kiaan looked to his mother, who nodded and smiled. Then he dashed upstairs to tell his sisters the good news.

***

After playing in the park, Kiaan and his family spent the rest of the day preparing for the week's festivities. Without a doubt, it was his most memorable *Diwali*.

Kiaan was glad to lend a helping hand during the festivities, and was happier to know that he was capable of pushing his limits. Tough challenges were easily conquered with a calm mind. All he had to do was relax, rethink, and breathe.

Down the Hill

It was a bright, sunny morning on the coast of Cape Town—perfect for a picnic by the sea.

Arno and his family drove across town to enjoy fresh air, watch the waves, and bask in nature. His mother packed a delicious lunch while his father prepared blankets and cushions. Arno and his older siblings, Jaco and Kayla, were in charge of bringing the entertainment. They loaded the trunk with water guns, beach balls, and frisbees. But even if there were many fun games to choose from, Jaco and Kayla were most excited to go biking across the hills. They gushed about how zooming down the trails felt like flying.

There was just one problem—Arno could hardly ride a bike.

CAPE TOWN

He spent the entire week practicing at home in the backyard. But whenever he made it past three pedals, he fell. Although his family encouraged him to take things slow and have fun, he always thought he would topple over again.

Standing on the hilltop with his bike, and a helmet strapped to his head made him even more jittery. He sighed, watching Jaco and Kayla race into the field.

"Come on, Arno! What are you waiting for?" called Jaco, his older brother.

"Don't keep us waiting," added Kayla, his sister.

Arno's palms began sweating as he tightly gripped his bike handles. He gulped, taking in the vast landscape. His breath hitched as he grew pale. Soon, he felt dizzy.

"I'm going to sit down for a while," he announced, dragging his bike toward a nearby tree.

"I'm never going to get this right," he grumbled, squatting under the shade.

Arno looked to the sky, feeling a little sorry for himself. He envied his siblings who cycled like pros. He tried to cheer himself up by drawing pictures on the ground with his finger. Just when he was about to finish, a twig fell on his shoulder.

Arno brushed it off. But two more followed. Before he knew it, a handful of leaves rained down on his head. Arno looked up, searching for what caused the ruckus. To his surprise, he spotted a young crowned eagle scrambling out of its nest.

The bird had long crested feathers tipped in white and a crown of black ones around its head. It had yellow feet, black talons, and a sharp beak. It stretched its magnificent wings and flapped them as it balanced itself on the branch.

Arno's eyes widened when he realized what the bird would do next.

"Don't fly! You'll hurt yourself!" Arno shouted.

But the fledgling ignored him. Instead, it inched closer to the edge of the tree.

Arno flushed with panic. He didn't want the bird to get hurt. He shot to his feet and scurried around the trunk, hoping to find a way up. To his delight, he found a sturdy rock to mount himself onto a low branch. Soon, he was off the ground.

"Stay where you are! I'll save you!" He screamed, climbing higher.

Arno was determined to reach the bird in time—he even kicked off his slippers halfway up the tree. Despite being high above the ground, he never looked down.

It doesn't know what falling feels like, he thought. *It isn't ready.*

When Arno finally arrived at the treetop, he carefully scooched toward the fledgling. But the moment the bird was within reach, it spread its wings and dove off the branch.

Arno's mouth hung wide as he watched the bird heading for the ground. But to his amazement, it beat its wings and lifted itself into the air. Arno marveled as he watched the young eagle soar into the sky and glide deeper into the forest.

That bird didn't even know if it could fly, he thought. *It just believed it could.*

Then an idea struck him.

Maybe that's what I need.

Arno quickly climbed down the tree. He took his bike to the hilltop, strapped on his helmet, and got in position. He tried to ignore his past blunders and focused on succeeding. Without wasting another second, he pushed himself forward.

Arno held the handles tightly as he pedaled down the hill. He kept his sights on the road and breathed steadily to keep his balance. As the sea breeze greeted him, he felt like he was on air. He smiled, grateful he saw the fledgling on its first flight.

Arno started getting the hang of things as he glided halfway down the slope. He couldn't help but proudly shout, "I'm doing it!" as he came to a sweet stop at the foot of the hill.

Arno's siblings watched from the sides and rushed toward him as he clutched on the brakes.

"That was great, Arno!" Jaco cheered.

"Amazing! How did you learn so fast?" Kayla asked.

Arno smiled, remembering the lesson of flight, fearlessness, and freedom he learned from an unlikely little teacher.

He turned to his siblings with a flicker of newfound confidence as he spoke.

"If a birdie believed it could fly before it could, I think I ought to believe in myself."

The Dental Treatment Delay

Walter Eriksson enjoyed everything about summertime in Sweden. In fact, it was his favorite season. He loved that the weather wasn't too hot, nor too cold, and that there was sunshine all day everyday. He longed to see the flowers in full bloom, hear the birds sing their merry tunes, and play outdoors with his friends. Plus, it meant that he had two months off from schoolwork.

Walter was especially looking forward to this year's vacation because his mother planned an exciting tour around the country. Little did he know that he had one more obstacle to get through before the big event.

"I've scheduled a dental appointment for you, dear," she said, lifting a pot of pea soup off the stove. "It's at one o'clock this afternoon."

Walter turned as pale as snow while watching her plate up lunch.

He had never been to the dentist before. In fact, he wished he never had to visit the dentist in his entire life! He heard horrible stories from his friends at school who said dentists loved collecting teeth. Walter was perfectly happy to keep his pearly whites snugly inside his mouth.

"But I feel fine, Mamma," he tried to reason.

Unfortunately, she already made up her mind.

"You don't have to be sick to go to the dentist, dear. This'll just be a quick checkup," she explained. "Now, come and eat your lunch. We don't want to be late."

Walter sulked as he looked down at his pea soup and pancakes, thinking of ways to escape this mess. His eyes brightened once he came up with the perfect plan.

I'm going to do all the household chores just in time for us to miss the appointment this afternoon, he thought.

He waited until after lunch to put his idea to the test.

As his mother started piling the dishes, Walter swooped in and took them in his arms.

He ran into the kitchen, saying, "Mamma, let me help you with that. You deserve a break! Just relax in the living room. I'll bring you some tea."

To his delight, his mother didn't suspect him of stalling. Instead, she thanked him for his thoughtfulness.

Walter stashed the dishes in the sink and turned on the tap. Then he switched the stove on, boiled some water, and prepared the teacup. When the kettle whistled, he poured water into the cup and picked out a packet of chamomile tea—the best choice for sleep and relaxation.

He ripped open the packet, dipped the tea bag into the liquid, and like a flash of lightning, he rushed to his mother in the living room.

"Here," he said, handing her the hot drink.

"That was quick," she answered, taking a sip. "Is this chamomile?"

It took a while for Walter to reply. "It's just something I pulled out from the drawer. I thought it smelled good."

He switched on the radio to some classical music. Then he collected all the pillows he could find and stuffed them behind his mother's back. He quickly pulled up a chair, hoisted her legs on his lap, and began rubbing circles on the soles of her feet.

"Walter, why are you acting strange?" his mother asked, yawning. "Are you done with the dishes?"

"Shhhh, Mamma. I'm trying to help you relax," he whispered. "Just close your eyes and listen to the music."

But she was persistent.

"Walter, we should get moving if you're done in the kitchen. We don't want to be late for—"

"Everything's perfectly fine, Mamma," Walter interrupted, hoping it would calm her nerves.

Unfortunately, he spoke too soon.

The fire alarm rang, causing them to spring to their feet. It was followed by a disturbing popping sound, then a loud crash. Their jaws dropped as they saw wisps of gray smoke coming in from the hallway. They hurriedly followed the trail into the kitchen.

Walter's mother couldn't help but shriek when she saw the place was a disaster.

The steel kettle rested on the stove, nearly swallowed by roaring flames. Its lid was missing. It had popped off, broke through the window, and landed outside. Shards of glass scattered across the countertop beside the sink, which was left running. It gushed like a waterfall over piles of dirty dishes, flooding half of the floor in tap water.

His mother shut the fire off before closing the sink. She hurriedly laid a bunch of kitchen towels over the wet floor. Then, she turned to Walter and demanded, "Explain all this!"

The boy bowed his head, feeling awful for his reckless mistake. He knew that hiding the truth from his mother would only make things worse. She deserved to know everything.

"I'm sorry," he said. "I was in a hurry to bring you tea. I wanted you to relax—and maybe fall asleep—so you'd forget about the dental appointment."

His mother ran her fingers through her hair and sighed, "Walter, are you frightened of going to the dentist?"

"I don't want him to take my teeth," he replied.

His mother crouched down to meet his eyes.

"Dental care is for your own good, honey," she said, smiling. "The dentist isn't going to hurt you."

"Do you promise?" Walter asked.

"I do," his mother assured.

Walter and his mother decided to clean the mess in the kitchen after the appointment. They rushed into the car, buckled their seatbelts, and soon they were on the road. They arrived at the dental office ten minutes early. After filling out a few forms, they went in to see the doctor.

The dentist was named Mr. Bergson. He was a lanky man who donned a long, white coat and shiny, black shoes. He had wild, blonde hair and wore a permanent smile on his face—which Walter thought was a funny sight. He asked Walter to tie an apron around his neck and sit on the patient's special chair.

Walter couldn't deny feeling a little excited as the seat reclined.

"Let's start by x-raying your teeth," Mr. Bergson said, handing Walter a small piece of plastic. "Please bite this."

Walter did as he was told. He watched as Mr. Bergson hovered a scanner outside his mouth. Walter was amazed to see his teeth through a monitor.

"Everything looks great," Mr. Bergson said, pulling a lamp above Walter's head. "Now, it's time for cleaning."

Walter leaned back and opened his mouth wide. His gums felt chilly when Mr. Bergson patted them with something called a dental probe. His teeth clanged lightly as the scaler scraped off plaque from his teeth. Walter felt ticklish as Mr. Bergson brushed his teeth with an electric toothbrush. To everyone's surprise, he giggled through the entire thing.

Finally, Walter was asked to gargle some water and apply fluoride gel on his teeth and gums. Then he was advised to brush his teeth two to three times a day to keep them strong and healthy.

"Good, strong bite. Teeth well aligned. No cavities. I'd say your first trip to the dentist was a success!" Mr. Bergson congratulated, shaking Walter's hand.

Then the dentist turned to Walter's mother to discuss the next appointment.

Walter realized that dental checkups were actually quite fun. He learned a lot about dental hygiene and was eager to keep his teeth clean and strong. He couldn't wait to tell his friends about how brave he was on his first visit. He also wondered whether something new might happen during the next dental appointment.

Before he knew it, he found himself tugging his mother's sleeve, whispering, "When can we visit again?"

The Feather of Truth

The Egyptian Museum of Ancient History proudly stood at the heart of Cairo. It was a magnificent building that shone heavenly under the Egyptian sun. Inside breathed with priceless treasures, causing locals and tourists to marvel in awe.

Little would anyone know that there was more to all that which met the eyes.

Today happened to be a very important day for Ramy and his class, who were visiting for the first time on a field trip. Ramy trailed behind, goggling at statues of ancient kings, queens, gods, and precious relics. He was having so much fun. He didn't want the day to end. He wanted to keep something as a reminder of this great adventure.

During the snack break, he spotted a box of trinkets at a souvenir shop. When nobody was looking, he picked a small golden scarab pin from the pile and stuffed it into his pocket. He felt a mixture of thrill and guilt as he rejoined his class. But chose not to tell anyone about what he stole.

As the class regrouped and headed toward the final showcase, Ramy felt his feet grow limp. He struggled to lift them, but the more he tried, the more they wouldn't budge. It didn't take long for the class to disappear into the hall. Soon, he was alone. To his horror, he started sinking into the ground. The poor boy was completely swallowed into the floor before he could call for help.

Ramy screamed as he fell into the darkness. He landed with a *clang* on a cold, metal surface. Suddenly, flames ignited the torches in all corners of the room. Ramy blinked, adjusting his vision to the light. He jerked back when he realized he was on the end of a large, golden scale. His eyes nearly shot out of their sockets when he saw what lay before him.

A giant goddess with hair as dark as night and ivory wings on each arm stood on a pedestal. She was dressed in a floor-length linen gown, ostrich feathers crowned her head. She turned to Ramy who shivered with fear.

In a deep, stirring voice she said, "I am Maat—goddess of truth and harmony. I see everything and know what lies deep in the hearts of men. You stole something, boy. For that you will face judgment."

"I didn't steal," Ramy fibbed. "I'm being honest."

Maat looked at him sternly. Ramy could sense she didn't believe him. There was a long moment of silence before the goddess stood up and spoke again.

"The scales will reveal the truth," she said, taking a feather from her hair and putting it on the pan at the opposite end of the scale.

"Truth, balance, order, harmony, law, morality, and justice—these are the virtues you must hold. Ramy, do you promise to speak the truth?" she asked.

Ramy nodded. Maat returned to the pedestal and gestured for him to tell his story.

"I didn't do anything wrong," he fibbed.

At that instant, Ramy dropped. He clung to the pan, trying to keep himself from slipping to the side.

"You are lying," Maat's thunderous voice echoed.

"It wasn't my fault! It was an accident!" Ramy cried.

It didn't make things any better. Instead, the beams tipped further in his direction. Ramy gasped when he looked over the edge to see a bottomless pit. He covered his ears to the horrible, painful screams of troubled souls in the darkness. As he descended, Ramy remembered the goddess's warning.

With all the courage he could muster, he looked Maat in the eyes and confessed.

"I was lying! I'm sorry!" He said, holding back his tears. "I stole a scarab pin from the souvenir shop. I just wanted to have something to remember this day."

Ramy cowered, afraid of being punished. But to his surprise, his pan lifted.

"You did the right thing," Maat said. "I release you."

Suddenly, Ramy felt as light as a feather. To his amazement, he started to float. As he rose to the ceiling, he saw the goddess vanish into thin air. Then everything turned black. His head spun as a strong gust of wind whirled him in circles. Like waking from a dream, he found himself lying on the cold museum floor.

Ramy stumbled toward the gift shop as soon as he regained his balance. Then he returned the scarab pin to the pile of souvenirs. He learned that stealing was wrong, and brought nothing but guilt and shame. From that moment on, he promised to always be truthful.

Still, he still wished for a token to remember the day.

Just when he thought he was going home empty handed, he felt prickling in his pockets. His eyes twinkled with delight as he pulled out a beautiful ostrich feather fan.

I CAN HELP OTHERS

www.ingramcontent.com/pod-product-compliance
Lightning Source LLC
Chambersburg PA
CBHW030305100526
44590CB00012B/525